CLIP ART

FOR YEAR C

STEVE ERSPAMER, SM

LITURGY TRAINING PUBLICATIONS

Duplicating the Art in This Book

The art in this book may be duplicated freely *by the purchaser* for use in a parish, school, community or other institution. This art may not be used on any materials that are intended to be sold.

CLIP ART FOR YEAR C

Copyright © 1994, Archdiocese of Chicago. All rights reserved.

Liturgy Training Publications
1800 North Hermitage Avenue
Chicago, Illinois 60622-1101

Order Phone: 1-800-933-1800
FAX: 1-800-933-7094
Editorial Offices: 1-312-486-8970

Editor: Victoria M. Tufano
Production editor: Deborah Bogaert
Designer: Kerry Perlmutter
Typesetter: Mark Hollopeter
Production: Roslyn Broder

Printed in the United States of America

ISBN 1-56854-035-3
$25.00

Table of Contents

Introduction

Opening this book is much like entering a great cathedral: Everywhere one turns, the great mysteries of the faith, the holy men and women of our tradition, and the symbols that have conveyed Christian hopes and beliefs from one generation to the next catch the eye, delight the heart and engage the mind. This book contains hundreds of delightful, engaging illustrations useful for bulletins, worship folders, calendars and handouts for each season and Sunday of the liturgical year.

About the Artist and the Art

Steve Erspamer is a Marianist brother who makes his home in St. Louis, Missouri. He is a many-faceted artist who works in clay, stone, fresco, art glass, silkscreened fabrics, block prints and, as this book demonstrates, cut paper.

Steve studied at St Mary's University in San Antonio, Texas; the Art Institute of San Antonio; Creighton University in Omaha; and Boston University. He has traveled in Western Europe and in India as a student of sacred art.

The artist brings to this book a respect for traditional iconography. In the positioning of the figures of Mary and the angel Gabriel, in the depicting of a parable, even in the drawing of an apple, there are customary styles in Christian tradition. These forms have evolved, in part, because of their beauty and elegance, but also, in part, as expressions of the gospel and as emblems of the reign of God.

Many of the images in this book have been drawn in the style of stone carvings in Romanesque churches that dot the great medieval pilgrimage route through France and Spain. This style, in turn, borrows from Byzantine iconography. As examples of this style, incidental characters often are pictured smaller than main characters; disciples show their allegiance to Jesus by bowing; sometimes a figure will bend and twist to fit a form. All of this gives to the style a peculiar earthiness and playfulness.

Decoration sometimes adds another layer of meaning— tame animals suggest a return to paradise; wild animals suggest the Spirit's gift of fortitude; roses are signs of the flowering of God's reign; pomegranates represent the fruitfulness of the kingdom of heaven.

Throughout this book on the pages facing the art are brief statements about the scriptures that the art represents. The Sunday's or feast's calendar date is included here. The scriptures of the Mass are listed.

Illustrations of the Sunday Readings

The book of scriptures read at the eucharist—the lectionary—is organized according to a few principles:

The first readings are most often from the books of the Jewish scriptures, what Christians call the Old Testament. But during Eastertime the first readings are from the Acts of the Apostles.

Second readings are read in sequence week by week through Ordinary Time. From the Second to the Eighth Sundays of Year C, we hear First Corinthians; from the Ninth to the Fourteenth Sundays, Galatians; from the Fifteenth to the Eighteenth Sundays, Colossians; from the Nineteenth to the Twenty-second Sundays, Hebrews; on the Twenty-third Sunday, Philemon; from the Twenty-fourth to the Twenty-sixth Sundays, First Timothy; from the Twenty-seventh to the Thirtieth Sundays, Second Timothy; from the Thirty-first to the Thirty-third Sundays, Thessalonians; and on the Thirty-fourth Sunday (Christ the King), Colossians. During the Easter season this year, the second readings are taken from Revelation.

Sunday gospels in Year C are most often from Luke. But on the Second Sunday in Ordinary Time, on the Third, Fourth and Fifth Sundays of Lent, and on most of the Sundays of Easter, the gospels are taken from John.

In this clip art book, all the first readings and gospel readings of Year C have been illustrated. If you need illustrations for the second readings, they're here, too, but they may take a bit of searching to find. For the second readings, a single piece of art can sometimes be used several Sundays in a row. The index can help you locate appropriate art for the second readings.

Preparing a Handout

Communications have become more visual and less verbal. Perhaps as a result of television, people are accustomed to complex visuals. They know when something looks unprofessional. That means that all of us who prepare bulletins, worship programs and the like are expected to produce sophisticated publications. That's hard work. It's skilled work, too, and it requires a sense of playfulness and creativity to do it well.

Here are a few hints: Allow yourself plenty of time to work on your project. Do the work as soon as you have all the necessary information; don't wait until the last minute. Something always goes awry: The copier needs toner, you run out of tape, you can't find a certain piece of music. Spare yourself some headaches.

Assemble your materials: Scissors, paper, tape or glue stick or wax stick (wax allows you to move pieces easily), ruler (a clear, flexible ruler with a grid marked on it is invaluable for laying things out straight).

Word processors are a great aid in producing nice-looking publications, especially with the aid of a good printer. Don't succumb to the temptation to use everything in your computer's bag of tricks on every project. Try not to mix typefaces; different sizes or degrees of boldness of the same typeface can be used instead. Instead of using the title of a song as it is printed with the music, type out the title and the copyright notices in the same typeface as the rest of the program. (If you use a lot of music from one publisher, create a macro on your word processor for their copyright notice. Include your reprint license number, if you have one.) Don't forget to include page numbers.

Be careful when mixing styles of art; it's hard to do this well. You may achieve a more professional look if you stick to one style. Be sure that all your pieces of art are clean and clear. Use correction fluid to get rid of any speckles, or find a clean copy.

Use blank "white space" liberally—not every available corner of a handout should be filled. As a rule, make sure both words and art have adequate space around them to give a clean look to the handout. Be sure to proofread your work, and have someone else proofread it as well. Take a second look at the appropriateness of the art. Typographical or grammatical errors or a confusing layout will make a handout far less inviting to read.

Investigate using unusual ink colors and papers; printers are happy to help, but be sure to ask about the extra cost, particularly of colored inks. When you choose ink and paper colors, remember that readability is the most important concern. There should be enough contrast between the ink and the paper to allow everyone to read the words, and the two colors together shouldn't make the eye "pop."

Emphasize the liturgical calendar in the parish bulletin, even if at times that means being at odds with other calendars. That might mean that Mother's Day gets a bit less attention than the season of Easter, that Valentine's Day gets no notice in years it falls right at the beginning of Lent, that the bulletin during Advent is free from Christmas images, and that during the Christmas season the bulletin keeps up the spirit even if the shops have called it quits.

Be conservative with words and liberal with art. For example, a worship folder cover need not state the obvious—"Christmas," or "Lent"—but be aware that these sometimes serve as mementos of special occasions. For anniversaries, ordinations, funerals, weddings or other such events, include the names of the principal persons involved and the date somewhere in the bulletin, but not necessarily on the cover.

Enlarge and reduce this art as needed. Many photocopiers can do this. The art in this book was fashioned from cut paper, which lends itself to the production of crisp enlargements and reductions. There is a point of diminishing returns, however: Be careful that the art is not reduced so much that it becomes undecipherable.

When preparing worship folders, try to enlarge words and music where appropriate—this can invite participation. Don't be afraid to make items as big as possible, as long as the whole is in scale.

You are free to copy the art in this book without acknowledgments if you use the art for a parish, school or other institution. However, you may not use this art (or any clip art) without written permission from the publisher if you sell the reproduction.

If you use a great deal of the art in this book through the year, please, at times, acknowledge the artist, the name of the book and the publisher. Users of parish and school handouts will appreciate the information. You may also consider, on occasion, providing explanations of the art you reproduce. Often it's helpful to call attention to art and, at times, to explain images that may be unfamiliar.

Liturgical images can educate as well as illustrate. They teach without words. They tell stories, evoke moods, and remind us of things we almost forgot. The images of this book do even more: They can lead us into the lectionary, into the scriptures and psalms, and even into the spirit of the liturgy. They can lead us into mystery.

Wisdom is a breath of the power of God,
and a pure emanation of the glory of the Almighty.
For she is a reflection of eternal light,
a spotless mirror of the working of God.

—*Wisdom of Solomon 7:25, 26*

Christ is the image of the invisible God,
the firstborn of all creation.

—*Colossians 1:15*

While our words and art forms
cannot contain or confine God,
they can, like the world itself, be icons,
avenues of approach, numinous presences,
ways of touching without totally
grasping or seizing.

—*Environment and Art in Catholic Worship, #2*

Works of art,
the most exalted expressions of the human spirit,
bring us closer and closer
to the divine Artisan.

—*Paul VI, 1979*

The liturgy must be human as well as divine.
It should have participation and it should have art.

—*Reynold Hillenbrand, 1962*

Advent Bulletin Cover

*Advent lasts from the fourth Sunday before
Christmas until the evening of Christmas Eve.*

November 27 to December 24, 1994
November 30 to December 24, 1997
December 3 to December 24, 2000

About the art: Advent is the time to pause, the time to
remember and celebrate that we are a people who
wait. As watch-keepers for the dawn, as a woman with
child, as Israel for the Messiah, Christians await the
coming of Jesus in glory, in the fullness of time. Come,
Lord Jesus!

Advent

First Sunday of Advent

violet

November 27, 1994
November 30, 1997
December 3, 2000

Jeremiah 33:14–16
Psalm 25
1 Thessalonians 3:12—4:2
Luke 21:25–28, 34–36

About the art: The Lord promises, through Jeremiah, to raise up for David a just shoot from the root of Jesse. The just shoot—the one who will do what is right—and the Sun of Justice are represented here. Jesus foretells the coming of the Son of Man on a cloud with great power and glory. Paul prays that we may overflow with love for one another.

See the art for the Solemnity of the Immaculate Conception on page 4. Francis Xavier, Jesuit missionary to India and Japan, is remembered on December 3. For an image of John Damascene (December 4) see page 28.

FRANCIS
XAVIER

Second Sunday of Advent

violet

December 4, 1994
December 7, 1997
December 10, 2000

Baruch 5:1–9
  Psalm 126
Philippians 1:4–6, 8–11
Luke 3:1–6

About the art: John the Baptist appears, crying out, "Make ready the way of the Lord." The prophet Baruch exhorts Jerusalem to shed its grief and to put on the glory of God, and Paul expresses his desire that we should be found rich in the harvest of justice.

Nicholas (December 6), bishop of Myra (now part of Turkey), is remembered for his generosity and his defense of the faith against Arianism. He is the patron of Russia and of children. Ambrose (December 7) was a catechumen, then bishop of Milan and a great teacher in the fourth century. He also wrote many hymns, including one honoring the bees for producing the wax for the paschal candle!

JERUSALEM TAKE OFF YOUR ROBE OF MOURNING

·AMBROSE·

JERUSALEM

NICHOLAS

MAKE STRAIGHT HIS WAY ·

Immaculate Conception

white

Thursday, December 8, 1994
Monday, December 8, 1997
Friday, December 8, 2000

Genesis 3:9–15, 20
  Psalm 98
Ephesians 1:3–6, 11–12
Luke 1:26–38

About the art: This feast celebrates Mary. Through her, the human race cooperated with God in overcoming sin, which came into the world when we cooperated with the serpent. All creation sings joyfully of the wonders that God has done for us.

5

Third Sunday of Advent

rose or violet

December 11, 1994
December 14, 1997
December 17, 2000

Zephaniah 3:14–18a
*   Isaiah 12:2–3, 4, 5–6*
Philippians 4:4–7
Luke 3:10–18

About the art: The Third Sunday of Advent was once called Gaudete (rejoice) Sunday, from the first word of the entrance antiphon for the day: "Rejoice in the Lord always; again I say, rejoice! The Lord is near" (Philippians 4:4, 5). This forms part of the second reading for today, too. In the first reading, Zephaniah exclaims, "Shout for joy, O daughter Zion!" John the Baptist exhorts us to prepare for the coming of the Lord by sharing with the poor and by acting justly.

Lucy (December 13), a Sicilian martyr whose name means "light," is honored in many places, especially Sweden, where girls wear candle-laden wreaths on their heads to serve breakfast in bed to their parents. Thomas (July 3) is remembered as the apostle who doubted, but he also brought the faith to India and died a martyr.

Joseph dreams of an angel who reveals to him that Mary is to be the mother of the savior. This story is read at the Christmas Vigil Mass.

Fourth Sunday of Advent

violet

December 18, 1994
December 21, 1997
December 24, 2000

Micah 5:1–4a
    Psalm 80
Hebrews 10:5–10
Luke 1:39–45

About the art: From Bethlehem shall come a ruler who will stand firm and shepherd his flock by the strength of the Lord. Mary visits her older cousin Elizabeth, who exclaims, "Blessed is she who trusted that the Lord's words to her would be fulfilled." The wisdom of God, personified as a woman in scripture, is pictured in the center image.

This is the last opportunity to print the Christmas schedule. Even if you've printed it before now, some people are sure to have lost it or never to have seen it. Reprinting it may save a lot of phone calls.

Christmas Season Bulletin Cover

The Christmas season lasts from the evening of Christmas Eve until the feast of the Baptism of the Lord.

December 25, 1994, to January 9, 1995
December 25, 1997, to January 11, 1998
December 25, 2000, to January 8, 2001

About the art: He shall be called Emmanuel, God with us.

Christmas

Christmas Day

white

Sunday, December 25, 1994
Thursday, December 25, 1997
Monday, December 25, 2000

Vigil

Isaiah 62:1–5
* Psalm 89*
Acts 13:16–17, 22–25
Matthew 1:1–25
* or Matthew 1:18–25*

Night

Isaiah 9:1–6
* Psalm 96*
Titus 2:11–14
Luke 2:1–14

Dawn

Isaiah 62:11–12
* Psalm 97*
Titus 3:4–7
Luke 2:15–20

Day

Isaiah 52:7–10
* Psalm 98*
Hebrews 1:1–6
John 1:1–18
* or John 1:1–5, 9–14*

Christmas Day requires our best efforts at hospitality. Many parishes prepare a handout to welcome the many people who come to worship on this day. This handout could also include prayers, songs and blessings for use at home. Extra copies of the schedule of services for the entire season might be made available for visitors.

Other art for Christmas Day can be found on pages 7, 9 and 10.

GOD WITH US

YOU HAVE NOTHING TO FEAR!

Sunday in the Octave of Christmas

white

Feast of the Holy Family
December 30, 1994
December 28, 1997
December 31, 2000

Sirach 3:2–6, 12–14
  Psalm 128
Colossians 3:12–17
  or Colossians 3:12–21
Luke 2:41–52

During Year C these readings may be used:
1 Samuel 1:20–22, 24–28
1 John 3:1–2, 21–24
Luke 2:41–52

About the art: Today's feast reiterates the message of Christmas: God's holy one dwells among and within human life. Don't exclude anyone today by including only stereotyped images—either verbal or written—of families.

An image of Stephen (December 26) and an image of John (December 27) are found on page 10.

Octave of Christmas

white

Mary, Mother of God
Sunday, January 1, 1995
Thursday, January 1, 1998
Monday, January 1, 2001

Numbers 6:22–27
   Psalm 67
Galatians 4:4–7
Luke 2:16–21

January 1, the Octave of Christmas, has many titles. On the Gregorian calendar, which most of the Western world follows, it is New Year's Day. On the Roman Catholic calendar, this day is "Mary, Mother of God," restoring the oldest Christian tradition that keeps this day as a feast of Mary. The day has also been named World Day of Prayer for Peace. In the Byzantine calendar, January 1 is the Circumcision of the Lord (the title in the Roman calendar before it was reformed after Vatican II). In the Lutheran and Episcopalian calendars, the day is the feast of the Holy Name of Jesus.

About the art: In the first reading, Aaron blesses the Israelites. The shepherds visit the child in the manger.

Stephen, the first martyr, is remembered on December 26. John (December 27) is remembered as the writer of the fourth gospel. His symbol, the eagle, adorns many pulpits.

Epiphany of the Lord

white

For Roman Catholics in the U.S.A. and Canada:
January 8, 1995
January 4, 1998
January 7, 2001

For other Christians:
Friday, January 6, 1995
Tuesday, January 6, 1998
Saturday, January 6, 2001

Isaiah 60:1–6
  Psalm 72
Ephesians 3:2–3a, 5–6
Matthew 2:1–12

Epiphany's traditional date is January 6, and many Christians throughout the world celebrate it on that date. In many Christian cultures, Epiphany is the day of gift-giving.

About the art: Epiphany means "revelation." Originally, the day celebrated many revelations of who Jesus is: his incarnation; his birth; and his manifestations to the Magi, the people gathered at the Jordan when Jesus was baptized by John, and the wedding guests at Cana. In the Catholic church, the story of the journey and adoration of the Magi is told.

Hilary (January 13) was bishop of Poitiers, France, in the fourth century. Simon Stylites (January 5) lived a life of asceticism, spending some of it living at the top of a pillar from which he exhorted people to change their ways and turn to God.

SIMON STYLITES

HILARY

Baptism of the Lord

white

Monday, January 9, 1995
Sunday, January 11, 1998
Monday, January 8, 2001

Isaiah 42:1–4, 6–7
   Psalm 29
Acts 10:34–38
Luke 3:15–16, 21–22

During Year C these readings may be used:
Isaiah 40:1–5, 9–11
Titus 2:11–14; 3:4–7
Luke 3:15–16, 21–22

About the art: This feast is a continuation of Epiphany and the conclusion of the Christmas season. Images of light and darkness, so prominent throughout this season, continue and are combined with baptismal images of water. Much of the art presented for today is also appropriate for celebrations of baptism.

MY FAVOR IS UPON HIM

JO HN

BAPT IZER

13

Winter Bulletin Cover

Tuesday, January 10, to Tuesday, February 28, 1995
Monday, January 12, to Tuesday, February 24, 1998
Tuesday, January 9, to Tuesday, February 27, 2001

About the art: The gospels at Sunday Mass during the segment of Ordinary Time between Christmas and Lent in year C—with the exception of the Second Sunday in Ordinary Time, when we read John's account of the miracle at Cana, another epiphany story—are taken from the early chapters of the gospel of Luke. On the Sixth Sunday, Psalm 1 declares that the one who meditates on the law of the Lord is "like a tree planted near running water . . . whose leaves never fade." The second readings for the Second to the Eighth Sundays are all from 1 Corinthians. For a piece of art good for all these Sundays, see page 18.

14

Second Sunday in Ordinary Time

green

January 15, 1995
January 18, 1998
January 14, 2001

Isaiah 62:1–5
Psalm 96
1 Corinthians 12:4–11
John 2:1–12

About the art: The wedding feast at Cana, another "epiphany," is recounted today. Isaiah tells downtrodden Israel that they shall be a glorious crown in the hand of the Lord. Paul praises the many gifts of the one Spirit.

Vincent (January 22) was a Spanish deacon who was martyred around the year 300. John Chrysostom (September 13) was a bishop and a wise preacher. He died in 407.

Art for the Martin Luther King, Jr., holiday is found on page 83.

PROPHECY

HEALING

WISDOM

FAITH

VINCENT

JOHN CHRYSOSTOM

DO WHATEVER HE TELLS YOU

15

Third Sunday in Ordinary Time

green

January 22, 1995
January 25, 1998
January 21, 2001

Nehemiah 8:2 – 4a, 5 – 6, 8 – 10
   Psalm 19
1 Corinthians 12:12 – 30
   or 1 Corinthians 12:12 – 14, 27
Luke 1:1 – 4; 4:14 – 21

About the art: Ezra reads from the scroll of the law, and the people shout "Amen!" Jesus reads from the scroll of the prophet Isaiah that announces glad tidings to the poor and release to prisoners. Paul reminds us that we are all the body of Christ.

For an illustration for the second reading, see page 18.

For an image of Thomas Aquinas, see page 25.

16

Fourth Sunday in Ordinary Time

green

January 29, 1995
February 1, 1998
January 28, 2001

Jeremiah 1:4–5, 17–19
   Psalm 71
1 Corinthians 12:31 — 13:13
   or 1 Corinthians 13:4–13
Luke 4:21–30

About the art: The prophet Jeremiah is promised that even though the kings and priests and people will fight him, they shall not prevail. Paul exhorts us to seek the greater gifts of faith, hope and love—especially love. Jesus proves again that prophets are never accepted in their own lands.

Francis de Sales (January 24) ministered with prudence and wisdom in the area around Geneva during the violent times of the Protestant Reformation. Margaret of Hungary (January 26) was the daughter of the king and queen of Hungary. Raised by a community of Dominican nuns from the age of three, she chose to practice asceticism to an extreme degree.

For an illustration for the second reading, see page 18.

MARGARET OF HUNGARY

FRANCIS de SALES

Presentation of the Lord

white

Thursday, February 2, 1995
Monday, February 2, 1998
Friday, February 2, 2001

Malachi 3:1–4
   Psalm 24
Hebrews 2:14–18
Luke 2:22–40
   or Luke 2:22–32

About the art: Through the prophet Malachi, the Lord promised, "I am sending my messenger to prepare the way before me; and suddenly there will come to the Temple the Lord whom you seek." In accordance with the Jewish law, Jesus was presented in the Temple 40 days after his birth, and two doves were sacrificed. On this day, also called Candlemas, candles are blessed to acclaim Christ the light of the world.

Brigid of Ireland (February 1) lived a life of service to the poor, founding convents to care for them. She is one of the patron saints of Ireland.

BRI
GID

18

Fifth Sunday in Ordinary Time

green

February 5, 1995
February 8, 1998
February 4, 2001

Isaiah 6:1–2a, 3–8
  Psalm 138
1 Corinthians 15:1–11
  or 1 Corinthians 15:3–8, 11
Luke 5:1–11

About the art: With the touch of a burning coal, the prophet Isaiah's lips are purified for his work. Jesus increases the fishermen's yield of fish and tells them that from now on it is people for whom they will fish. The image in the upper right corner may be used for all the Sundays on which Corinthians is read.

Sixth Sunday in Ordinary Time

green

February 12, 1995
February 15, 1998
February 11, 2001

Jeremiah 17:5–8
  Psalm 1
  1 Corinthians 15:12, 16–20
  Luke 6:17, 20–26

About the art: Those who hope in the Lord are like trees planted near a stream, bearing fruit even in times of distress. Jesus preaches the blessedness of the poor and oppressed, and the woefulness of the self-satisfied. Paul reminds us that Christ is the first of those to be raised from the dead. For another illustration of the second reading, see page 18.

Juliana (February 16) suffered torture and eventual martyrdom by her father and suitor for refusing to marry. Legend says that Juliana fought with the devil, who tried to persuade her to comply with their wishes. She is usually pictured binding the devil.

JULIANA

20

Seventh Sunday in Ordinary Time

green

February 19, 1995
February 22, 1998 (Sunday before Ash Wednesday)
February 18, 2001

1 Samuel 26:2, 7–9, 12–13, 22–23
   Psalm 103
1 Corinthians 15:45–49
Luke 6:27–38

About the art: David refuses to kill his sleeping enemy, Saul. Jesus teaches us to love our enemies and to bless those who maltreat us. Paul notes that just as we resemble the first Adam, so shall we bear the likeness of Jesus, the second Adam.

Matthias (May 14) was chosen as the apostle to replace Judas. Like most of the apostles, he died a martyr's death. Serenus (February 23) was a fourth-century ascetic who lived in and tended an enclosed garden. He was martyred for being a Christian during the reign of the emperor Maximian.

SERENUS

Eighth Sunday in Ordinary Time

green

February 26, 1995 (Sunday before Ash Wednesday)
February 25, 2001 (Sunday before Ash Wednesday)

Sirach 27:4–7
Psalm 92
1 Corinthians 15:54–58
Luke 6:39–45

About the art: Just as a the proof of the quality of a pot is in the furnace (Sirach), and the proof of the tree is in its yield, so the proof of what is in the human heart is in a person's speech (gospel). In Jesus' victory, death has been robbed of its power.

See pages 18 for art for the second reading.

Ninth Sunday in Ordinary Time

green

1 Kings 8:41–43
Psalm 117
Galatians 1:1–2, 6–10
Luke 7:1–10

About the art: Solomon prays that the Lord will hear
the prayers of all, even the foreigner, so that the Lord's
name will be blessed by all peoples. Jesus finds faith in
a foreigner, a Roman centurion, and answers his peti-
tion. Paul reminds us that no one—not even an angel
from heaven—may change the gospel of Christ.

Lent Bulletin Cover

Lent lasts from Ash Wednesday until the celebration of the Evening Mass of the Lord's Supper on Holy Thursday.

Ash Wednesday, March 1, to Holy Thursday, April 13, 1995
Ash Wednesday, February 25, to Holy Thursday, April 9, 1998
Ash Wednesday, February 28, to Holy Thursday, April 12, 2001

About the art: In Lent we prepare to renew the promises of our baptism and to witness and celebrate the vows of those who will be baptized at Easter. Each year, on the second Sunday of Lent, an account of the Transfiguration is proclaimed. It foreshadows the glory of the resurrected Christ, into whose life we are baptized.

24

Ash Wednesday

violet

March 1, 1995
February 25, 1998
February 28, 2001

Joel 2:12–18
*   Psalm 51*
2 Corinthians 5:20—6:2
Matthew 6:1–6, 16–18

About the art: "Call an assembly! Proclaim a fast!" today's scriptures demand—and so we do. We begin Lent with a reminder to return to the Lord, just as the people of Israel did with prayers and sacrifices. Jesus reminds us that our prayer, fasting and almsgiving must be done simply, not as a show for others.

Blessed Henry Sosu (March 2) was a Dominican friar, preacher, writer and prior. He lived in Germany, where he died in 1365. Aelred (March 3) was a twelfth-century Cistercian of the monastery of Rievaulx in Yorkshire, England. He wrote of friendship, both divine and human.

AELRED

ON SPIRITUAL FRIENDSHIP

THE BOOK OF ETERNAL WISDOM

HENRY SUSO

First Sunday of Lent

violet

March 5, 1995
March 1, 1998
March 4, 2001

Deuteronomy 26:4–10
  Psalm 25
Romans 10:8–13
Luke 4:1–13

About the art: Moses instructs the people to offer their gifts at the altar and to remember who they were and what the Lord had done for them. Following Jesus' baptism, the Holy Spirit leads Jesus into the desert to face the devil.

Frances of Rome (March 9) was a wife, a mother and the founder of a religious community. Thomas Aquinas (January 28) was a great teacher and theologian of the Dominican order.

FRANCES OF ROME

AQUINAS

26

Second Sunday of Lent

violet

March 12, 1995
March 8, 1998
March 11, 2001

Genesis 15:5–12, 17–18
  Psalm 27
Philippians 3:17—4:1
  or Philippians 3:20—4:1
Luke 9:28b–36

About the art: Abraham makes a covenant with God, who promises that his descendants shall be as numerous as the stars in the sky. Paul exhorts us to stand firm in the Lord. The glory of the risen Lord—and of all the baptized—is foreseen in his transfiguration.

Patrick (March 17) was an evangelizer and bishop of Ireland. Gregory the Great (September 3) was a pope and an esteemed teacher. Louise de Marillac (March 15) founded, with Vincent de Paul, the Sisters of Charity of St. Vincent de Paul.

27

Third Sunday of Lent

violet

March 19, 1995
March 15, 1998
March 18, 2001

Exodus 3:1–8a, 13–15
   Psalm 103
1 Corinthians 10:1–6, 10–12
Luke 13:1–9

The readings of Year A may be used on this Sunday, especially when the scrutinies are celebrated:
Exodus 17:3–7
   Psalm 95
Romans 5:1–2, 5–8
John 4:5–42
   or John 4:5–15, 19b–26, 39a, 40–42

About the art: The Lord speaks to Moses from the burning bush, instructing him to lead the Israelites to their own land. The fig tree that bears no fruit will be cut down.

Joseph, the husband of Mary, is remembered on two days, March 19 and May 1.

28

Fourth Sunday of Lent

rose or violet

March 26, 1995
March 22, 1998
March 25, 2001

Joshua 5:9a, 10–12
   Psalm 34
2 Corinthians 5:17–21
Luke 15:1–3, 11–32

*The readings of Year A may be used on this Sunday,
especially when the scrutinies are celebrated:*
1 Samuel 16:1b, 6–7, 10–13a
   Psalm 23
Ephesians 5: 8–14
John 9:1–41
   or John 9:1, 6–9, 13–17, 34–38

About the art: After arriving in the promised land, the
Israelites celebrated the Passover and ate unleavened
bread and parched grains. Jesus tells those around
him that God welcomes back sinners and tax collectors
like a father welcomes back a prodigal son. Paul reminds
us that we are new creations in Christ.

The Feast of the Annunciation (March 25) marks the
beginning of the incarnation. Benedict, whose feast
day is July 11, is also celebrated in Benedictine communities on March 21. He is remembered as the Father
of Monasticism. John Damascene (December 4) was
a painter of icons and a composer of hymns.

BENEDICT

WHEAT

JOHN OF DAMASCUS

29

Fifth Sunday of Lent

violet

April 2, 1995
March 29, 1998
April 1, 2001

Isaiah 43:16–21
   Psalm 126
Philippians 3:8–14
John 8:1–11

The readings of Year A may be used on this Sunday, especially when the scrutinies are celebrated.
Ezekiel 37:12–14
   Psalm 130
Romans 8:8–11
John 11:1–45
   or John 11:3–7, 17, 20–27, 33b–45

About the art: Just as the Lord opened a path in the sea, says Isaiah, so the Lord will make a way in the desert. Jesus dispels a crowd that would stone a woman who was caught in adultery, and then he admonishes her to sin no more. Nearing the end of his ministry, Paul compares himself to a runner with his eyes on the finish line.

According to legend, Mary of Egypt (April 2) lived during the fifth century and repented of her dissolute life by living an ascetic life in the wilderness beyond the Jordan River. Benedict the Black (April 4) was born of African slaves in Sicily in the sixteenth century. After joining the Friars Minor as a lay brother, he became well-known for his holiness and wisdom. He served as religious superior and as spiritual advisor to people of all stations in life. He is the patron of the Black peoples of North America.

MARY OF
EGYPT

BENEDICT THE BLACK

30

Passion (Palm) Sunday

red

April 9, 1995
April 5, 1998
April 8, 2001

Procession:
   Luke 19:28–40

Isaiah 50:4–7
   Psalm 22
Philippians 2:6–11
Luke 22:14—23:56
   or Luke 23:1–49

About the art: The events we remember on Palm Sunday—Jesus' triumphal entry into Jerusalem, a woman washing Jesus' feet and anointing his head, and Jesus' trial, torture, death and burial—are a profound meditation on Jesus' life and on the meaning of life for all who would follow him.

31

Triduum Bulletin Cover

The Paschal Triduum of the death, burial and resurrection of the Lord lasts from the celebration of the Mass of the Lord's Supper on Holy Thursday until sundown Easter Sunday.

Holy Thursday, April 13, to Easter Sunday, April 16, 1995
Holy Thursday, April 9, to Easter Sunday, April 12, 1998
Holy Thursday, April 12, to Easter Sunday, April 15, 2001

About the art: The Triduum, the most solemn time for Christians, is one three-day commemoration during which the events of Jesus' life from the Last Supper to the Resurrection are celebrated as one great mystery.

Triduum

32

Holy Thursday Evening

white

April 13, 1995
April 9, 1998
April 12, 2001

Exodus 12:1–8, 11–14
   Psalm 116
1 Corinthians 11:23–26
John 13:1–15

About the art: This evening, the story of the Passover of the Jews from slavery to freedom begins the telling of the story of Jesus' Passover—and ours—from death to life, which we celebrate throughout the Triduum.

See page 47 for other images appropriate for today.

33

Good Friday

red

April 14, 1995
April 10, 1998
April 13, 2001

Isaiah 52:13—53:12
   Psalm 31
Hebrews 4:14–16; 5:7–9
John 18:1—19:42

About the art: Today we remember and venerate the cross of Jesus, the suffering servant of God. Other images of the cross and passion of Christ are on pages 30, 50 and 67.

THIS IS MY SERVANT

34

Easter Vigil

white

April 15, 1995
April 11, 1998
April 14, 2001

Genesis 1:1 — 2:2
  or Genesis 1:1, 26 – 31a
    Psalm 104
    or Psalm 33
Genesis 22:1 – 18
  or Genesis 22:1 – 2, 9a,
  10 – 13, 15 – 18
    Psalm 16
Exodus 14:15 — 15:1
    Exodus 15
Isaiah 54:5 – 14
    Psalm 30
Isaiah 55:1 – 11
    Isaiah 12
    or Psalm 51

Baruch 3:9 – 15, 32 — 4:4
    Psalm 19:8 – 11
Ezekiel 36:16 – 17a,
  18 – 28
    Psalms 42 and 43
    or Isaiah 12
    or Psalm 51
Romans 6:3 – 11
    Psalm 118
Luke 24:1 – 12

About the art: The story of God's relationship to humankind is retold this night, from the creation to the resurrection, to our own death and resurrection in the waters of baptism. Other baptismal images can be found on pages 12 and 57.

CHRIST YESTERDAY & TODAY

WHY DO YOU SEARCH FOR THE LIVING ONE AMONG THE DEAD.

35

Easter Season Bulletin Cover

The Easter season lasts from Easter Sunday until Pentecost Sunday.

Easter Sunday, April 16, to Pentecost, June 4, 1995
Easter Sunday, April 12, to Pentecost, May 31, 1998
Easter Sunday, April 15, to Pentecost, June 3, 2001

About the art: By his death he has forever conquered death, Alleluia!

EASTER

36

Easter Sunday

white

April 16 1995
April 12, 1998
April 15, 2001

Acts 10:34a, 37–43
  Psalm 118
Colossians 3:1–4
  or 1 Corinthians 5:6b–8
John 20:1–9
  or Luke 24:13–35 (evening Mass)

About the art: The stone is rolled away; the tomb is empty. The great joy of the other apostles spills out into the preaching of the good news.

37

Second Sunday of Easter

white

April 23, 1995
April 19, 1998
April 22, 2001

Acts 5:12–16
  Psalm 118
Revelation 1:9–11a, 12–13, 17–19
John 20:19–31

About the art: Thomas comes to believe by touching the wounded, risen body of Christ. Through faith in him, the apostles healed the sick. John has a revelation of the Son of Man surrounded by seven lampstands.

For an image of Thomas, see page 5.

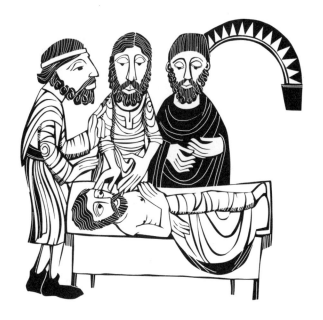

38

Third Sunday of Easter

white

April 30, 1995
April 26, 1998
April 29, 2001

Acts 5:27–32, 40b–41
   Psalm 30
Revelation 5:11–14
John 21:1–19
   or John 21:1–14

About the art: The Risen Lord appears to those assembled at the Sea of Tiberias and shares a meal of bread and fish. The apostles are questioned by the Sanhedrin and forbidden to preach Jesus' name. John envisions the throng around the throne, praising the Lamb.

For another image of Joseph (May 1) see page 27. St. Michael is remembered on September 29, along with the other archangels found in scripture, Gabriel and Raphael.

JOSEPH
THE
WORKER

39

Fourth Sunday of Easter

white

May 7, 1995
May 3, 1998
May 6, 2001

Acts 13:14, 43–52
   Psalm 100
Revelation 7:9, 14b–17
John 10:27–30

About the art: Today is sometimes called Good Shepherd Sunday because the gospels for the Fourth Sunday of Easter, always from John, deal with passages about shepherds and sheep. In the first reading, Paul and Barnabas preach at the synagogue in Antioch and are driven out; so they shake the dust from their feet and go on. John sees a throng of every race, dressed in white robes and holding palm branches, gathered before the throne.

Juliana of Norwich (May 13) was a mystic and a spiritual counselor who wrote of the mystery of God's love.

40

Fifth Sunday of Easter

white

May 14, 1995
May 10, 1998
May 13, 2001

Acts 14:21–27
   Psalm 145
Revelation 21:1–5a
John 13:31–33a, 34–35

About the art: At several churches, Paul and Barnabas encourage their disciples and install elders. John sees a vision of the new heavens, the new earth and the new Jerusalem. Jesus gives his disciples a new command: love one another.

St. John Nepomucen (May 16) is a patron of Bohemia. He was a priest who served as vicar general of his diocese and was martyred in 1393 for helping to preserve the goods of a monastery from the devious actions of the king. On the night he was killed by being thrown from a bridge, legend says that seven stars hovered over the water.

Rita of Cascia (May 22) became an Augustinian after the deaths of her husband and two sons, all of whom had been violent men. She lived the rest of her days in humility, dying in 1457. She is often pictured with roses; legend says that on her deathbed she requested a rose from her garden. Even though it was out of season, roses were found blooming there.

For an image of Matthias (May 14), see page 20.

HOLY JERUSALEM

JOHN NEPOMUK

RI TA

41

Sixth Sunday of Easter

white

May 21, 1995
May 17, 1998
May 20, 2001

Acts 15:1–2, 22–29
  Psalm 67
Revelation 21:10–14, 22–23
John 14:23–29

About the art: Paul, Barnabas, Barsabbas and Silas are sent from Judea to Antioch to assure the people that no undue burden will be placed on them. An angel carries John away to see the new Jerusalem. Jesus promises to send the Paraclete.

Bernardino of Siena (May 20) was a fifteenth-century Italian preacher. Madeleine Sophie Barat (May 25) founded the Society of the Sacred Heart, in nineteenth-century France, for the education of girls.

BERNARDINO OF SIENA IHS

BARNABAS PAUL JUDAS SILAS

JERUSALEM

MADELEINE SOPHIE

42

Ascension of the Lord

white

In the U.S.A.:
Thursday, May 25, 1995
Thursday, May 21, 1998
Thursday, May 24, 2001

In Canada:
Sunday, May 28, 1995
Sunday, May 24, 1998
Sunday, May 27, 2001

Acts 1:1–11
  Psalm 47
Ephesians 1:17–23
  or Hebrews 9:24–28; 10:19–23
Luke 24:46–53

About the art: Jesus commissions the Eleven to make disciples of all nations and to baptize them. Then he ascends to his place at God's right hand, where he reigns in majesty over all the earth.

Augustine (also called Austin) of Canterbury (May 27) evangelized Britain in the sixth century. Joan of Arc (May 30), in the fifteenth century, heard heavenly voices that directed her to fight to restore the throne of France to its rightful heir.

JOAN OF ARC

AUSTIN

OF
CANTERBURY

THIS JESUS WILL RETURN TO YOU.

43

Seventh Sunday of Easter

white

May 28, 1995
May 24, 1998
May 27, 2001

Acts 7:55–60
   Psalm 97
Revelation 22:12–14, 16–17, 20
John 17:20–26

In Canada, this Sunday is observed as the Solemnity of the Ascension of the Lord.

About the art: Stephen, the first to die for his faith, sees a vision of Jesus at the right hand of God. For this, onlookers stoned him to death. John hears the voice of Jesus, the Root of Jesse, the Morning Star. We await the coming of the Holy Spirit.

Kevin (June 3) was an abbot and an ascetic; he is a patron of Dublin.

STEPHEN

VENI SANCTE SPIRITUS

44

Pentecost

red

June 4, 1995
May 31, 1998
June 3, 2001

Vigil

Genesis 11:1–9
   or *Exodus 19:3–8a, 16–20b*
   or *Ezekiel 37:1–14*
   or *Joel 3:1–5*
   Psalm 104
Romans 8:22–27
John 7:37–39

Day

Acts 2:1–11
   Psalm 104
*1 Corinthians 12:3b–7,
12–13*
   or *Romans 8:8–17*
John 20:19–23
   or *John 14:15–16,
23–26*

About the art: In one of the readings of the Vigil, the prophet Joel says that the spirit of the Lord will be poured out—the young will see visions and the old will dream. On Pentecost day, the Spirit is poured out like fire on those gathered, and they begin to prophesy. Jesus bestows the Spirit on the disciples, giving them the power to bind and loose.

45

Summer Bulletin Cover

Ordinary Time—"counted" time—resumes with evening prayer on Pentecost Sunday. But two Sunday feasts, Trinity Sunday and the Solemnity of the Body and Blood of Christ, occur before we settle into the long green period.

In the Northern hemisphere, Ordinary Time resumes in the late spring. The summer months are filled with signs of life (crops in the fields and orchards, children and families at play) and death (floods and drought, holiday traffic deaths, urban violence). During this time, the church remembers the lives and deaths of John the Baptist, Peter and Paul, Mary the Mother of Jesus and, at every eucharist, Jesus. The memory of the cross of Christ is celebrated in a special way on the feast of the Triumph of the Holy Cross on September 14, about the time that summer begins to turn to autumn.

SUMMER

Trinity Sunday

white

June 11, 1995
June 7, 1998
June 10, 2001

Proverb 8:22–31
Psalm 8
Romans 5:1–5
John 16:12–15

About the art: When the earth was formed, Wisdom was there, playing before God. Jesus tells us that when the Spirit of truth comes, we will be guided to all truth.

Body and Blood of Christ

white

June 18, 1995
June 14, 1998
June 17, 2001

Genesis 14:18–20
  Psalm 110
1 Corinthians 11:23–26
Luke 9:11b–17

About the art: Melchizedek honored God with a sacrifice of bread and wine. Jesus feeds the masses, beginning with five loaves and two fish and ending with twelve baskets of leftovers. Paul tells us that every time we eat the bread and drink the cup, we proclaim the death of the Lord.

Anthony of Padua (June 13) taught theology and preached while living a life of total poverty. According to legend, Alban (June 22) was the first to be martyred for the faith in the British Isles.

ANTHONY

ALBAN

EVERY TIME YOU DO THIS YOU PROCLAIM THE DEATH OF THE LORD

Tenth Sunday in Ordinary Time

green

1 Kings 17:17–24
Psalm 30
Galatians 1:11–19
Luke 7:11–17

About the art: Elijah restores the son of the widow to life. Jesus, too, revives a widow's son. Paul, after several years of ministry to the Gentiles, goes to Jerusalem to become acquainted with Peter.

Eleventh Sunday in Ordinary Time

green

2 Samuel 12:7–10, 13
   Psalm 32
Galatians 2:16, 19–21
Luke 7:36—8:3 or 7:36–50

About the art: Nathan rebukes David for spurning all
that the Lord has done for him and doing evil. A
woman washes Jesus' feet with her tears and anoints
him with expensive perfume. Rather than rebuke
her, he compares her to those who have been released
from great debt. Paul declares that because he has
been crucified in Christ, Christ now lives in him.

50

Twelfth Sunday in Ordinary Time

green

June 25, 1995

June 21, 1998

Zechariah 12:10–11; 13:1

Psalm 63

Galatians 3:26–29

Luke 9:18–24

About the art: Zechariah prophesies that on the day the spirit is poured out on Jerusalem, her people shall weep over her. One day while Jesus is praying alone, he asks the disciples who they say he is. Then he instructs them about what it means to follow him. Because of our faith in Christ Jesus, each of us is a son or daughter of God.

WHO DO YOU SAY I AM

YOU ARE THE MESSIAH

51

Birth of John the Baptist

white

Saturday, June 24, 1995
Wednesday, June 24, 1998
Sunday, June 24, 2001

Vigil	**Day**
Jeremiah 1:4−10	*Isaiah 49:1−6*
Psalm 71	*Psalm 139*
1 Peter 1:8−12	*Acts 13:22−26*
Luke 1:5−17	*Luke 1:57−66, 80*

About the art: The Lord places his word in the mouth of his servant. Zechariah names his son John, just as the angel told him to do. John becomes a sharp-edged sword, a polished bow (Isaiah), proclaiming repentance and announcing the coming of another.

Thirteenth Sunday in Ordinary Time

green

July 2, 1995
June 28, 1998
July 1, 2001

1 Kings 19:16b, 19–21
Psalm 16
Galatians 5:1, 13–18
Luke 9:51–62

About the art: While plowing, Elisha hears the call to be a prophet from Elijah. Jesus tells a would-be follower that the Son of Man has nowhere to lay his head. Paul enjoins those freed by Christ not to take on the yoke of slavery again.

John Fischer was a bishop and Thomas More was chancellor of England. Both were martyred for refusing to accept the king as head of the church. They are remembered together on June 22.

THOMAS
MORE

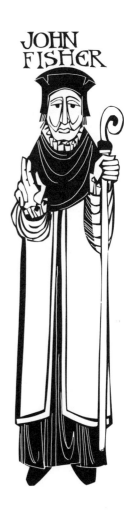

JOHN
FISHER

53

Sts. Peter and Paul

red

Thursday, June 29, 1995
Monday, June 29, 1998
Friday, June 29, 2001

Vigil	**Day**
Acts 3:1–10	*Acts 12:1–11*
Psalm 19:2–5	*Psalm 34*
Galatians 1:11–20	*2 Timothy 4:6–8, 17–18*
John 21:15–19	*Matthew 16:13–19*

About the art: An angel of the Lord releases Peter from prison. Peter holds the keys of authority. Paul is symbolized by the book of the word of God and the sword of martyrdom, and Peter is symbolized by the rooster that crowed after his third denial of Christ.

Legend says that when Veronica (July 12) wiped the face of Jesus with her veil, his image was imprinted on it.

Illustrations for Independence Day and other national days are on page 83.

VERONICA*

54

Fourteenth Sunday in Ordinary Time

green

July 9, 1995
July 5, 1998
July 8, 2001

Isaiah 66:10–14
   Psalm 66
Galatians 6:14–18
Luke 10:1–12, 17–20
   or Luke 10:1–9

About the art: As a mother comforts her child, so will Jerusalem comfort her children. Psalm 66 directs us to sing God's praises. Jesus sends out seventy-two disciples in pairs, as lambs among wolves. Paul asserts that he bears the marks of Jesus on his body.

For an image of the apostle Thomas (July 3) see page 5. Illustrations for Independence Day and other national days are on page 83.

55

Fifteenth Sunday in Ordinary Time

green

July 16, 1995
July 12, 1998
July 15, 1998

Deuteronomy 30:10–14
   Psalm 69
Colossians 1:15–20
Luke 10:25–37

About the art: Moses admonishes the people to keep the Lord's commands. The Good Samaritan is a neighbor to one who should be his enemy. In Jesus Christ, the firstborn of all creation, all things have their being.

For an image of Benedict (July 11), see page 28. Mary Magdalene (July 22) was the "apostle to the apostles." She followed Jesus to his death and was the first to proclaim his resurrection.

56

Sixteenth Sunday in Ordinary Time

green

July 23, 1995
July 19, 1998
July 22, 2001

Genesis 18:1–10a
   Psalm 15
Colossians 1:24–28
Luke 10:38–42

About the art: Abraham offers hospitality to three men at Mamre. Martha and Mary each respond to the Lord's presence in her own way. This image of Paul preaching may be used for all Sundays when Colossians is read.

John Cassian (July 23), who founded monasteries in Marseilles and wrote important works on monastic life, was a disciple of John Chrysostom. Ann is the mother of Mary and the grandmother of Jesus. Along with her husband, Joachim, she is remembered on July 26.

CASSIAN

ANNE

COLOSSIANS

57

Seventeenth Sunday in Ordinary Time

green

July 30, 1995
July 26, 1998
July 29, 2001

Genesis 18:20–32
Psalm 138
Colossians 2:12–14
Luke 11:1–13

About the art: Jesus teaches his disciples to pray with persistence, like someone seeking a favor in the middle of the night. Abraham persistently bargains with God for the survival of Sodom and Gomorrah.

Ignatius of Loyola (July 31) began as a Spanish soldier. He ended up as the founder of the Society of Jesus and a teacher of a way of prayer.

These baptismal images may be used throughout the year. A generic image for the second reading is found on page 56.

58

Eighteenth Sunday in Ordinary Time

green

August 2, 1998
August 5, 2001

Ecclesiastes 1:2; 2:21–23
   Psalm 95
Colossians 3:1–5, 9–11
Luke 12:13–21

About the art: Qoheleth and Jesus warn us not to labor at piling up wealth, for eventually we all die. What we must seek is the glory of God. Psalm 95 reminds us that God is our shepherd. A generic image for the second reading is found on page 56.

Dominic (August 8) founded the Order of Preachers, or the Dominicans, to preach against heresy. The dedication of the Church of SS. Peter and Paul in Rome is remembered on August 1. The church was said to house the chains that St. Peter wore in prison.

59

Transfiguration of the Lord

white

Sunday, August 6, 1995
Thursday, August 6, 1998
Monday, August 6, 2001

Daniel 7:9–10, 13–14
    Psalm 97
2 Peter 1:16–19
Luke 9:28b–36

About the art: The prophet Daniel has a vision of the Ancient One on the throne and of the son of man receiving dominion, glory and kingship. Jesus is transformed before Peter, James and John, and takes his place with Moses and Elijah. The Second Letter of Peter says we should attend to the message, "This is my beloved Son," as we would to a lamp in the darkness. For other appropriate art for this day, see page 26.

Clare (August 11) was a friend and follower of Francis of Assisi. She established the women's communities of Franciscans. Her name means *light.*

CLARE

60

Nineteenth Sunday in Ordinary Time

green

August 13, 1995

August 9, 1998

August 12, 2001

Wisdom 18:6–9

  Psalm 33

Hebrews 11:1–2, 8–19

  Hebrews 11:1–2, 8–12

Luke 12:32–48

  or Luke 12:35–40

About the art: By faith God's people have awaited the salvation of the Just. By faith Abraham went where he was sent and Sarah conceived Isaac when she was old. Jesus instructs his followers to wait in faith for the master's return.

Roch (August 17) was a Frenchman who tended the victims of plague while on pilgrimage to Rome. When he contracted the disease himself, he secluded himself in the woods so that he would die without being a burden to anyone. A dog found him there and fed him. He survived and continued to minister to the sick. Helen (August 18) was the mother of the emperor Constantine and the finder of the True Cross. Bernard (August 20) was a preacher, an abbot and a monastic reformer in the twelfth century.

HELEN

BERNARD

ROCH

61

Assumption of Mary

white

Tuesday, August 15, 1995
Saturday, August 15, 1998
Wednesday, August 15 2001

Vigil	**Day**
1 Chronicles 15:3–4, 15–16;	*Revelation 11:19a;*
16:1–2	*12:1–6a, 10ab*
Psalm 132	*Psalm 45*
1 Corinthians 15:54b–57	*1 Corinthians 15:20–26*
Luke 11:27–28	*Luke 1:39–56*

The feast of the Assumption recalls many images of Mary: the maiden visited by an angel; the young pregnant woman visiting her older, pregnant cousin; the woman clothed with the sun, a sign in opposition to the seven-headed dragon; the Ark of the Covenant that bore God's word; and the faithful believer who shares in Christ's victory over death.

NOW HAVE
SALVATION &
POWER COME

62

Twentieth Sunday in Ordinary Time

green

August 20, 1995
August 16, 1998
August 19, 2001

Jeremiah 38:4–6, 8–10
   Psalm 40
Hebrews 12:1–4
Luke 12:49–53

About the art: Jeremiah's preaching so angers the rulers that they throw him in a cistern. Psalm 40 rejoices that the Lord has saved us from the mud and put a new song into our mouths. Jesus foretells that he will cause dissension, pitting parents against children. But we should not despair; Jesus has triumphed over death and is enthroned at the right hand of God.

The memorial of the Immaculate Heart of Mary may be celebrated on the Saturday after the solemnity of the Sacred Heart. Moses is commemorated in the Byzantine calendar on September 4.

63

Twenty-first Sunday in Ordinary Time

green

August 27, 1995
August 23, 1998
August 26, 1995

Isaiah 66:18–21
Psalm 117
Hebrews 12:5–7, 11–13
Luke 13:22–30

About the art: Isaiah prophesies that people of all lands will be gathered by the Lord. The Letter to the Hebrews notes that the Lord disciplines those whom he loves. Jesus cautions that not everyone who knocks at the master's door will be admitted.

Rose of Lima (August 23), the first saint canonized from the Americas, lived a life of service to the poor. The beheading of John the Baptist is commemorated on August 29. After the defeat of the Spanish Armada, the English government resumed its persecution of Catholics. Several men and women were put to death, beginning on August 28; they are known as the martyrs of London of 1588.

ROSE OF LIMA

MARTYRS OF LONDON

64

Twenty-second Sunday in Ordinary Time

green

September 3, 1995
August 30, 1998
September 2, 2001

Sirach 3:17–18, 20, 28–29
  Psalm 68
Hebrews 12:18–19, 22–24a
Luke 14:1, 7–14

About the art: Sirach notes that alms atone for sin, as a water quenches fire. Jesus teaches the proud to humble themselves, taking the lowest places rather than the highest. The mountain of God, the heavenly Jerusalem, is a place of festivity.

Peter Claver (September 9) was a priest who spent most of his life serving the black slaves in Colombia. Hildegard of Bingen (September 17) was a twelfth-century abbess, physician, writer, preacher, musician and spiritual guide. Her writings reveal a particular regard for nature. For an image of Gregory the Great (September 3), see page 26.

PETER
CLAVER

ALMS

HILDEGARD
OF BINGEN

65

Twenty-third Sunday in Ordinary Time

green

September 10, 1995
September 6, 1998
September 9, 2001

Wisdom 9:13–18b
   Psalm 90
Philemon 9–10, 12–17
Luke 14:25–33

About the art: "Who ever knew your counsel," the book of Wisdom asks, "except you had given Wisdom and sent your holy spirit?" Paul writes to Philemon from prison. Jesus asks, "Does not someone who wants to build a tower first calculate to see if there is enough money to complete the project?"

Matthew (September 21) was an apostle whose name has been given to one of the four gospels. He had been a Galilean tax-collector. Francis of Assisi (October 4) received on his body the marks of the Lord's passion.

YOU SENT YOUR SPIRIT FROM ON HIGH.

MATTHEW

66

Twenty-fourth Sunday in Ordinary Time

green

September 17, 1995
September 13, 1998
September 16, 2001

Exodus 32:7–11, 13–14
  Psalm 51
1 Timothy 1:12–17
Luke 15:1–32
  or Luke 15:1–10

About the art: Even though the people of Israel worshiped a god of their own making, the Lord did not destroy them. God is like a father who welcomes home a prodigal child, like a woman who diligently seeks a lost coin, like a shepherd who seeks a lost sheep. Paul offers praise "to the king of ages, the immortal, the invisible." Psalm 51 asks God to open our lips that our mouths may praise God.

For an image of John Chrysostom (September 13), see page 14. Joseph of Cupertino (September 18) was a Capuchin who was said to have prayed so fervently that he often levitated. Columba (September 27) was put to death in 853 by the Moors in Spain for her Christian faith.

THE KING OF AGES BE HONOR GLORY

O LORD OPEN MY LIPS

COLUMBA

67

Triumph of the Cross

white

Thursday, September 14, 1995
Monday, September 14, 1998
Friday, September 14, 2001

Numbers 21:4–9
  Psalm 78
Philippians 2:6–11
John 3:13–17

About the art: Today's feast evokes many images of the cross: a glorious, jewelled cross; an Ethiopian cross; and a cross from which springs a fountain of life-giving waters. The saving cross of Christ is prefigured by the serpent mounted on the pole, which saved the Israelites from death by snakebite in the desert.

Theodore (September 19) was a Russian duke who, with his sons David and Constantine, is honored as a model Christian and nobleman. Forced to marry for the sake of political alliance, Catherine of Genoa (September 15) devoted herself to prayer, the care of the sick and the writing of mystical works.

68

Autumn Bulletin Cover

Ordinary Time continues through the autumn, as we settle back into the routines of work and school, as the days grow shorter and colder, and as the green fields turn gold and then brown. Our thoughts turn toward our own end. We celebrate Halloween to look in the face of death and fear—and laugh. In Mexican communities, the *Día de los Muertos* reminds us that death is part of life and that the dead are still with the living, just as the living will one day be with the dead. As Christians, we remember our beloved dead, especially at the beginning of November. And we will remember them all month as we look forward in faith to the time when everything we know will come to an end and Christ will reign in the fullness of God's kingdom.

AUTUMN

69

Twenty-fifth Sunday in Ordinary Time

green

September 24, 1995
September 20, 1998
September 23, 2001

Amos 8:4–7
  Psalm 113
1 Timothy 2:1–8
Luke 16:1–13
  or Luke 16: 10–13

About the art: The prophet Amos warns dishonest merchants who cheat the poor. Paul urges us to offer petitions, prayers, intercessions and thanksgivings for all. And Jesus asserts that no one can serve two masters.

Theresa of the Child Jesus (October 1), a Carmelite sister, is revered for the simplicity of her faith. Francis of Assisi is remembered on October 4. For another image of Francis, see page 65. Bruno (October 6) was an eleventh-century priest who founded the Carthusian order.

THERESE

BRUNO

70

Twenty-sixth Sunday in Ordinary Time

green

October 1, 1995
September 27, 1998
September 30, 2001

Amos 6:1a, 4–7
   Psalm 146
1 Timothy 6:11–16
Luke 16:19–31

About the art: Jesus tells of the rich man who ignores the poor beggar Lazarus until it is too late.

The archangels Michael, Gabriel and Raphael (September 29) are celebrated as messengers, protectors, intercessors and companions. For another image of Raphael, see page 73; for one of Michael, see page 77.

71

Twenty-seventh Sunday in Ordinary Time

green

October 8, 1995
October 4, 1998
October 7, 2001

Habakkuk 1:2–3; 2:2–4
  Psalm 95
2 Timothy 1:6–8, 13–14
Luke 17:5–10

About the art: The prophet Habakkuk writes down the vision given him by the Lord. If we had faith, the Lord says, we could order the sycamore to uproot itself, and it would. The psalm invites us to sing joyfully to God, our shepherd.

Bridget (July 23) is the patron of Sweden, remembered for her passion for justice and her concern for the poor.

Teresa of Jesus (October 15) was a Carmelite mystic and reformer. Her writings on the spiritual life are the foundation for all later teachings.

72

Twenty-eighth Sunday in Ordinary Time

green

October 15, 1995
October 11, 1998
October 14, 2001

2 Kings 5:14–17
   Psalm 98
2 Timothy 2:8–13
Luke 17:11–19

About the art: Elisha cures Naaman in the Jordan River, an image that may call to mind our baptism. Jesus cures ten lepers, and one returns to give thanks. Paul suffers imprisonment for the word of God. For an illustration of the second reading, see page 71.

Luke (October 18) is the writer of both the gospel that bears his name and the Acts of the Apostles. He is often symbolized by a bull.

73

Twenty-ninth Sunday in Ordinary Time

green

October 22, 1995
October 18, 1998
October 21, 2001

Exodus 17:8–13
Psalm 121
2 Timothy 3:14—4:2
Luke 18:1–8

About the art: While Moses prayed with his arms upraised, the Israelites were victorious over the army of Amalek. The persistence of the widow in petitioning the unjust judge teaches us about the need for constant prayer. Paul notes that the sacred scriptures are the source of all wisdom. For an illustration of the second reading, see page 71.

Raphael is remembered on September 29, along with the other archangels (see page 70). Anthony Claret (October 24) founded the Claretians in Spain in the nineteenth century for the work of preaching retreats and writing. He was also a bishop in Cuba.

ANTHONY
CLARET

RAPHAEL

74

Thirtieth Sunday in Ordinary Time

green

October 29, 1995

October 25, 1998

October 28, 2001

Sirach 35:12–14, 16–18

  Psalm 34

2 Timothy 4:6–8, 16–18

Luke 18:9–14

About the art: The Pharisee and the tax collector each go to the Temple to pray. Sirach tells us that the Lord hears the cry of the oppressed. Paul reflects on the race he has run. For another illustration of the second reading, see page 71.

Simon and Jude (October 28) were apostles of the Lord. Little is known of their ministry, but tradition says that they died as martyrs in Persia (Iran).

HE HEARS THE CRY OF THE POOR

SIMON JUDE

75

Thirty-first Sunday in Ordinary Time

green

November 5, 1995
November 4, 2001

Wisdom 11:22—12:2
   Psalm 145
2 Thessalonians 1:11—2:2
Luke 19:1–10

About the art: Before the Lord the whole universe is as a grain from a balance. Zaccheus climbs a tree to get a better look at Jesus. And Psalm 145 tells us that the Lord lifts up all who are falling.

Charles Borromeo (November 4) was a learned bishop. For another image of him, see page 77. Martin of Tours (November 11) was a soldier who left the military to follow the Lord. He later became bishop. Albert the Great (November 15) was a teacher of Thomas Aquinas. He is also a patron of education. Gertrude (November 16) was a mystic who had a vision of the throne of God.

THE LORD LIFTS UP ALL WHO ARE FAILING

CHARLES BORROMEO

MARTIN

ALBERTUS MAGNUS

GERTRUDE

76

All Saints

white

Wednesday, November 1, 1995
Sunday, November 1, 1998
Thursday, November 1, 2001

Revelation 7:2–4, 9–14
Psalm 24
1 John 3:1–3
Matthew 5:1–12a

About the art: The feast of All Saints calls forth images of the end-time: the Lamb, the throne surrounded by angels and saints, the saints dressed in white. In John's vision, an elder asks him who all the people in white are. The palm branch and the crown are symbols of the victory of the reign of God. In the beatitudes, Jesus calls the peacemakers "children of God."

77

All Souls

black, violet or white

Thursday, November 2, 1995
Monday, November 2, 1998
Friday, November 2, 2001

Readings for All Souls can draw from any of the readings for the Masses for the Dead.

About the art: The images of All Souls Day combine remembrance of the beloved dead with hope of their—and our—resurrection. The women are greeted at Jesus' tomb by angels who tell them that he is not there. Michael the archangel is the guardian of the people. At the end of time, the Son of Man will separate the sheep from the goats.

Martin de Porres (November 3) was a Peruvian of mixed race who served the poor and the sick of all races. See page 75 for another image of Charles Borromeo (November 4).

MARTIN
DE PORRES

MICHAEL GUARDIAN
OF THE PEOPLE

CHARLES
BORROMEO

HE IS NOT HERE
HE HAS BEEN RAISED

78

Thirty-second Sunday in Ordinary Time

green

November 12, 1995
November 8, 1998
November 11, 2001

2 Maccabees 7:1–2, 9–14
  Psalm 17
2 Thessalonians 2:16—3:5
Luke 20:27–38
  or Luke 20:27, 34–38

About the art: The Sadducees try to trip Jesus up with a trick question regarding the resurrection. A Maccabean mother and her sons show faith and courage in the face of death.

The daughter of a king and the wife of a nobleman, Elizabeth of Hungary (November 17) lived a life of prayer and charity. After the death of her husband, she continued her work as a sister of the Third Order of St. Francis. Little is known for sure of Catherine of Alexandria (November 25), but because tradition says she converted many by her speech, she is the patron of Christian philosophers, preachers, apologists and women students. John of the Cross (December 14) was a priest, a mystic and a writer of spiritual literature.

ELIZABETH
OF HUNGARY

JOHN OF THE CROSS

CATHERINE OF ALEXANDRIA

79

Dedication of the Lateran Basilica

white

Thursday, November 9, 1995
Monday, November 9, 1998
Friday, November 9, 2001

Any readings from the common for the dedication of a church may be chosen.

About the art: This is the dedication anniversary of the cathedral of Rome, the "mother church" of Roman Catholics. Images drawn from the many options for readings include Solomon before the altar, a sparrow finding a home on God's altar, people reconciling before offering their gifts, the ark of the covenant, the heavenly Jerusalem and an angel carrying incense.

80

Thirty-third Sunday in Ordinary Time

green

November 19, 1995
November 15, 1998
November 18, 2001

Malachi 3:19–20a
  Psalm 98
2 Thessalonians 3:7–12
Luke 21:5–19

About the art: The prophet Malachi tells of the coming of the sun of justice with its healing rays. Jesus says that many signs—plagues, earthquakes and fearful signs in the sky—will precede the time of tribulation. Paul makes a rule that only those who work may eat.

81

Christic the King

white

Last Sunday in Ordinary Time
November 26, 1995
November 22, 1998
November 25, 2001

2 Samuel 5:1–3
Psalm 122
Colossians 1:12–20
Luke 23:35–43

About the art: The elders of Israel anoint David King of Israel. Jesus, crucified below a sign reading "The King of the Jews," was raised from the dead and enthroned in the heavens.

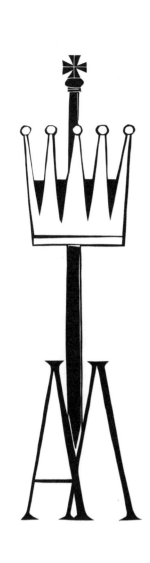

82

Thanksgiving Day

white

In Canada,
the second Monday in October:
October 10, 1995
October 13, 1998
October 9, 2001

In the U.S.A.,
the Fourth Thursday in November:
November 23, 1995
November 26, 1998
November 22, 2001

Readings may be chosen from the weekday; from the Masses for various public needs, "After the Harvest" or "In Thanksgiving"; or from the votive Mass for Thanksgiving Day.

About the art: Some of the images suggested by the readings include Jesus curing a leper, all the earth blessing God, and Jesus instructing the man who had been exorcised of a demon to go home and tell his family what the Lord had done for him.

GO TELL HOW MUCH THE LORD HAS DONE FOR YOU

LET ALL YOUR WORKS GIVE YOU THANKS

ALL THE KINGS OF THE EARTH GIVE THANKS TO YOU

O LORD

83

National Days

Martin Luther King, Jr., Birthday
January 15,
observed on the third Monday in January

Lincoln's Birthday
February 12

Presidents' Day
Third Monday in February

Washington's Birthday
February 22

Victoria Day (Canada)
Third Monday in May

Memorial Day
Last Monday in May

Canada Day
July 1

Independence Day
July 4

Labor Day
First Monday in September

Columbus Day
October 12,
observed on the second Monday in October

Election Day (U.S.A.)
First Tuesday after the first Monday in November

Veteran's Day
November 11

Remembrance Day (Canada)
November 11

ONE NATION UNDER GOD.

84

Index